Volume

CHARSFIELD
AND SURROUNDING
DISTRICT
IN PICTURES

Produced by PEGGY COLE

Best Wishes
Peggy Cole

PUBLISHED BY
THE FIVE CASTLES PRESS LIMITED

ACKNOWLEDGEMENTS

TO THE PEOPLE who have helped me with the photographs – Peter Driver, R. Bassett, Alan Randall, Alan Buckles, Phyllis Mapperley, Margaret Spall, C. Miller, C. Warne, B. Husk, Daphne Archer, L. Parker, M. Davy, K. Birch, K. Chapman, I. Stebbings, R. Durrant, H. Backhouse, N. Dickerson, S. Frost, D. and J. Grant, B. and J. Cole, M. Mayhew, D. Murray, V. Short and A. Anderson, Rev M. Bateman, R. Taylor, R. Havers, S. Fletcher, Mrs Goudy, P. Peck and the *East Anglian Daily Times*. I am indebted to Iris Stebbings for helping me to prepare and list the photographs for this book and to Beverly Gugenheim for help with typing. My thanks also to The Five Castles Press for their valuable assistance in this publication.

My thanks to Peter Driver for his Foreword to this book.

ISBN 0 9535830 2 3

Published by The Five Castles Press Limited, Raeburn Road South, Ipswich, Suffolk IP3 0ET
Set and printed by The Five Castles Press Limited

INTRODUCTION

AFTER THE FIRST book *"Charsfield and Surrounding District in Pictures"* was published, I had so many kind comments and was asked if I was doing another book. With the help of friends I have used the remaining photographs left over from the previous book. I find that people do love old photos and they do create a lot of interest. This time I have many photos from outside Charsfield, such as Waldringfield where my mother was born and many, past and present, were given to me by my nephew, Norman Dickerson. I have spent many pleasant hours playing on the sands at the River Deben.

In putting the book together, I notice that many of the lovely old houses in our area have disappeared. Some of the photographs which I have taken leave me with a feeling of nostalgia.

ABOUT THE AUTHOR

PEGGY was born in 1935, the eldest of a large Suffolk family. Her parents were landworkers in Easton, where Peggy was brought up. This hard beginning in life did not discourage her, in fact it provided the foundation stone for a love affair with her rural Suffolk.

In 1953 Peggy married Ernie Cole, a stockman. They had two sons, Allan and David, who are both now married and have five children between them. Peggy and Ernie began married life at Hoo. After a short stay at Kesgrave they moved to Charsfield.

At their council house in Charsfield they began to create a remarkable cottage garden. Tragically, Ernie died suddenly in 1980, but Peggy carried on her hard work in the garden with help from her brother Ronnie.

Peggy has published four other books and a commercial video has been made of her garden.

Peggy closed her garden to the public in 1997 due to ill health. This had been open for 25 years and had raised over £65,000 for various charities.

Peggy played a major role as the mother in the television adaptation of Ronald Blythe's *Akenfield*, and has given several hundred lectures on Akenfield and her garden, in Britain, the USA and on the QE2. However, failing health has reduced the frequency of these. Peggy writes a column in the *East Anglian Daily Times* each week and has a slot on BBC Radio Suffolk.

In 1992 Peggy was awarded an MBE in recognition of her charity work.

Peggy is never happier than when she is at home in her beloved Suffolk pottering in her garden.

FOREWORD

THE SECOND HALF of the twentieth century saw radical changes to country living. The availability of the motor car to people on moderate incomes and the electrification of the railway service to London reduced the isolation of the county. Where a trip of twenty miles had been a great adventure to someone living in Charsfield or Monewden before the war, it now became commonplace. This allowed men and women, replaced by labour-saving machinery introduced to farms, to seek employment elsewhere and more affluent town dwellers, looking for a different way of life, to purchase cottages as the amenities improved.

Where once a "Suffolker" had rarely heard the Mother Tongue spoken in any other dialect than his own, his ears were assailed by "Middle English" via the radio and television and other regional accents as the nation's workforce became more mobile. The effect has been a watering down of the Suffolk dialect, for to speak as your grandparents did assumes ignorance, resulting in many natives shedding their regional voice, if not the intonation.

I think it is fair to assume that village life as Peggy remembers it is gone, never to return and that is by no means a bad thing. Many of the photographs she has painstakingly assembled in this, her second collection, show people who lived a hard life. The lines on their weather-beaten faces tell of days spent soaking wet and freezing cold, with few of the "luxuries" we take for granted today. If we could ask them which way of life they would prefer they would think a while before settling on the comfort of the twenty-first century tempered with the contentment and human qualities of earlier times.

Like all good recorders, Peggy includes modern photographs in this collection along with the old. As each day finishes, all that has happened during it becomes history and someone in the future will bless her for her work and determination to ensure that the way of life of our rural Suffolk parishes in the twentieth century is not forgotten.

Peter Driver

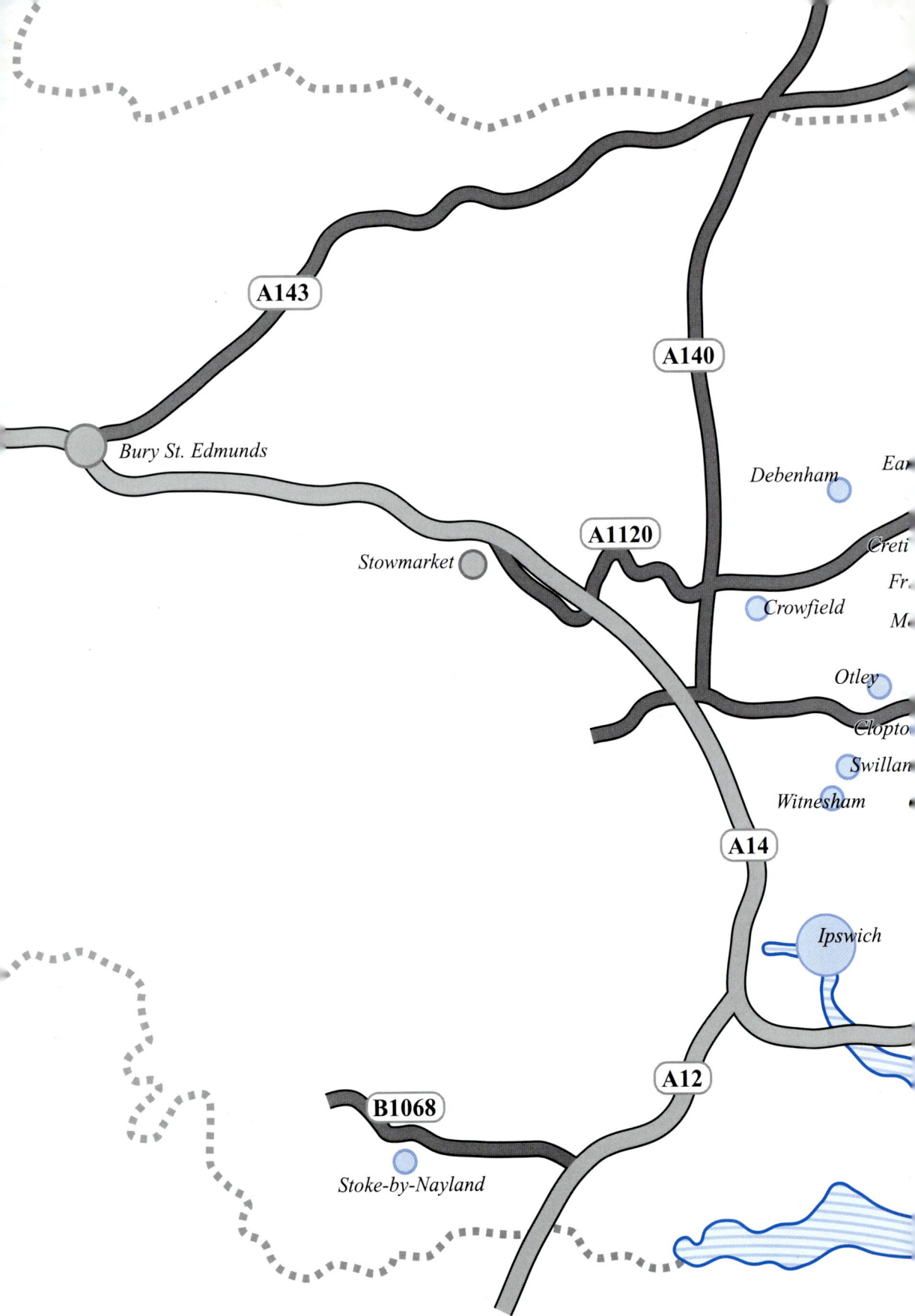

A143

A140

Bury St. Edmunds

Debenham

Ea

Creti

A1120

Crowfield

Fr.

M.

Stowmarket

Otley

Clopto

Swillan

Witnesham

A14

Ipswich

A12

B1068

Stoke-by-Nayland

A12

Walpole

A1120

Framlingham

B1119

Saxmundham

Leiston

Brandeston

Kettleburgh

Easton

Hoo

■ Glevering Hall

Blaxhall

Aldeburgh

Wickham Mkt.

Campsea Ashe

Sudbourne

Pettistree

Dallinghoo

B1078

Boulge

Bredfield

Wantisden

Burgh

Melton

isburgh

Woodbridge

A12

Martlesham

Waldringfield

Hemley

Ramsholt

Bawdsey

A14

otley

Felixstowe

Post Corner, Charsfield, before 1934

Amy and Leonard Havers outside village store, 1935

Amy, Richard, Robert and Leonard Havers

Building Charsfield council houses (late 1940s)

Tubby Crane, Peggy Keen, Nellie Goudy, Jack Branton (left), George Goudy (right)

Sidney Randall and family, 1974

30th April 1924, marriage of George Padfield and Marjorie Western, Charsfield – outside Park Farm, Charsfield

Jepthah Hart, Chapel Lane, Charsfield (late 1940s). Well-known nurseryman

Edna Buckles, Kenny Chapman, Faith Fryett. (Girl on right unknown)

Pastor Viner and Sunday School, Charsfield

Roger Handley and Allan Randall hoeing sugar beet

Rev Martyn Bateman, Vicar of Charsfield, and children Mary and John, early 1960s

Group in the Charsfield Three Horseshoes – publican "Mac" on right

Church outing, Charsfield – G. Mead, E. Cole, T. Harris, K. Chapman, V. and D. Mead,
E. Balls

Church outing, Charsfield, in Rev D. W. Ellis-Jones' time – E. Cole, K. Chapman, M. Fryett and family

Amos (Ace) Davy on Ipswich Road, Charsfield

Charsfield Girls' Brigade with Mrs Adelaide Fox, Mrs Pam Peck and Miriam Buchanan

Girl Guides, Bredfield, 1946

Charsfield Boys' Brigade, Spring 1983

Three generations of Boys' Brigade, Davy family, Charsfield

George Mead with E. Cole, B. Cole and J. Cole

Mrs P. Mapperley's Saplings Club (a children's club which used to meet each week and do useful jobs) at Charsfield

Mrs P. Mapperley's Saplings Club

Cynthia Mapperley, Saplings Club, being presented to Princess Anne. Mrs Mapperley on right

Saplings Club

Floods, Charsfield Street, May Bank Holiday 2000. Joe Garner and his sister, Megan

Floods at Little Brook (Mr Evans), Charsfield 2000

Confirmation – Bishop Dr Leslie Brown at Pettistree Church, May 1966

Monewden Choir in early 1950s

Well Farm, Charsfield, present time

The changing scenes of one house – Well Farm, Charsfield, 1947

Well Farm, Charsfield, 1948

Well Farm, Charsfield, 1953

Fred Johnson, Janice Brown, Leslie Thorndike, Hubert Smith and Brian Harvey, 1954

Charsfield Cricket Club, 1878, Captain: Rev Macgachan

Digging out the fish pond at Glevering, near Wickham Market, 1906

Resting on a "Rolls Royce" at Monewden, 1927, Kirby Branton

Mary Whiting and Leslie Pilkington

Tom Whiting's mother

Tom and Mary Whiting – wedding

Horace Holland, Maurice and Emily Mayhew

Fred and Annie Green who used to live at Brook Farm, Dallinghoo

George Mayhew who also used to live at Brook Farm

Maurice Mayhew's mother, Emma. Tea party at Brook Farm

Mr and Mrs David Hunt and Phoebe Brown, Monewden

Pastor Baker's son, Henry, and his wife, who now live in the USA. Visited the author in 2000

Roger Handley and Julie Branton

John Robert Spall and Constance (née Holland), 1913, outside The Oval, Dallinghoo

Cable carrier built at Blake's. John Spall stands behind

The saw-yard behind garage, Dallinghoo. Leslie Spall as a small boy

Mr Andrew Blake

George Anderson with Joe Arbon and "Gem", Bredfield

Garage and wheelwright's, 1923, Dallinghoo. Leslie Spall with wheelbarrow

Three generations of Spall family: John Robert (right), Leslie John (left) and Derek in front of his father

St Audry's Hospital, Melton

St Audry's Hospital, Melton

St Audry's Melton – Whitwell House

The "new" St Audry's with old tower, now called Melton Park

St Audry's Hospital, Melton, Milden and Melford Wards

St Audry's Chapel

Sunday School teachers' meeting led by Rev J. C. Titcombe, Woodbridge, 1905

Queen Victoria's Diamond Jubilee – Committee for Woodbridge celebrations

Beech tree at Melton traffic lights . . .   *. . . Beech tree cut down, August 2000*

Chapel at Melton being removed boldily from original site in 1861

Shire Hall, Woodbridge

No 100 Seckford Street, Woodbridge

The Abbey, Woodbridge

Woodbridge Fire Service

The crew of 493rd Bomb Group 861 rst Squadron Station 152 from Debach

Bawdsey Manor

Roger Clark's farm, Stoke-by-Nayland

Horseshoes at Roger Clark's farm

Drinking in the Bredfield Castle

The Neale brothers, Bredfield (William and Percy) plus uncles George and William

Mr and Mrs Percy Neale's Golden Wedding

Bredfield School, 1947

Bredfield Home Guard

Dallinghoo netball team, 1950

Jack Backhouse, Dallinghoo

Jack Backhouse and Albert Warner, Bredfield

Clopton Crown, Mr B. Birch delivering meat with horse and cart

Bredfield Hall, 1949, now demolished

Boulge Hall, now demolished

Maurice Shimmen holding plaque in memory of Edward Fitzgerald, Boulge

Plaque on garden wall at Bredfield, Edward Fitzgerald's birthplace

Miss V. Short and Miss J. Atkinson at the Fitzgerald family mausoleum in Boulge Churchyard – next to Edward Fitzgerald's grave

Boulge Church

Debach Church – now made into a house

Monewden Church

Monewden Hall, home of the Gooderham family (late 1920's)

Swilland Church

Crowfield Church

Walpole Old Chapel

Inside Walpole Old Chapel

Wantisden Church

Gyrotiller, Power of the Past at Wantisden

Wickham Market Bridge Floods, 1939

Leiston Abbey

Campsea Ashe Church

The Bridge & Ford, Martlesham.

Bridge and ford, Martlesham

The Street, Martlesham

Wilford Bridge, Melton

Waldringfield Beach (Author's mother and great aunts)

Loading Barges, Waldringfield.

Loading barges, Waldringfield

Aldeburgh, Three Mariners Inn

The Deben, Waldringfield

Waldringfield Church

Celebration of 100 years of the Waller family, at Hemley, 1999. The Right Rev Richard Lewis, Bishop of St Edmundsbury and Ipswich

Churchwarden, David Sterry in background, presenting gift to Rev John Waller at Hemley

Waldringfield ladies on a cycle ride

Waldringfield School, 1951

Waldringfield School, 1950

Waldringfield Village Road

The Post Office, Waldringfield

The Old Post Office, Waldringfield

Harness makers' shop. Grundisburgh, Mr G. Reeve

Grundisburgh Hall

The Green and School, Grundisburgh

Grundisburgh School

Jimmy Smy and Ernie Wardley with horse and cart. They used to sell oil and hardware in the Blaxhall and Snape area

Bob Smy at drawing match, Blaxhall

Mr and Mrs Puttock, Blaxhall

Johnnie Cole and Frank (Tooter) Crane

Blaxhall Church. In front, George Smith, shepherd to James Toller

Martlesham Brook and Red Lion

Burgh Mill

Brandeston Hall

Earl Soham Victoria Inn

Brandeston Street

Earl Soham Street

Herbert Moss, Meadows Cottages, Monewden, 1927

Mrs May Somers – Edna's mother

Mrs Sally Moss, née Buckles, Meadows Cottages, Monewden

The Yews, Brandeston, about 1910

John Emeny and Arthur Branton about 1910

Earl Soham school gardens, early 1900s

The Grundisburgh Bus, Model "T" Ford of the early 1920s

Rev Joshua Davies

William and Mary Ann Durrant and daughter Margaret, 1869

William Durrant with sons-in-law James Saunders and Nathan Minter, May 1913

Schemer Jessup

Mrs M. Simper, Mrs A. Havers and
Mrs G. V. Turner

Mrs Evelyn Kitson, Mrs M. Simper and
Mrs A. Havers

Mrs Hill, Kettleburgh, feeding her chickens
at The Chequers

Hangman's Post, Potsford Wood, Wickham
Market

Fred Reach with Chevrolet

Herbert Read and Fred Reach (on left)

Schemer Jessup on bumper and Mick Chittock on top (with cap)

Fred Reach with Model "T" Ford

Debenham

Low Street and Church, Cretingham

River Orwell, Ipswich

Brandeston Low Street

Rev H. Macgachen with Monewden bellringers, early 1920's

Rev Hugh Macgachen and daughter, Margaret, 1902 Ford

George Thorndike, Monewden

Margaret Macgachen and her mother

Willy Thorndike, Harry Moss and Jack Taylor, Monewden

Mrs H. Osborne, Mrs Gertie Read and Mrs Florrie Crane (sisters-in-law), Charsfield

Ocean, Alice and Adolphus Harris who lived at Magpie Street, Charsfield

Mrs Jeannie Shipp and daughter, Joan, who lived next to the Chapel

Mrs Alice Johnson and friend (kept sweetshop in The Street, Charsfield)

John Balls (author's grandfather) coming home from work at Kettleburgh

Cottages at Ramsholt

The Old Weighing Machine, Woodbridge

The Randall family, Charsfield, 1910

Mr and Mrs G. Goudy outside Buttons Farm, Charsfield

Nurse Gilson and Miss M. Woolnough

Jake and Bob Chapman (pre-1914) at Stanway Cottages – now Kiln Farm, Hoo

Charles, Jacob, Emin & Kenneth Chapman, 1932 Charsfield

Jake Chapman (on tractor) and Tom Whiting (on binder) at Youngman's farm

Jake Chapman (on tractor) and Bob Chapman

Harvesting at Witnesham, July 1952

Harvesting at Hoo Hall, 1930s

Clifford Arbon as a young man

Jimmy and Olive Green, Charsfield

Ernie Balls (Author's uncle) working on his bread round

Charsfield School, 1930s

New Street School, Woodbridge

Charsfield Chapel

New Chapel Hall, Charsfield, opened September 2000

The Vicarage, Charsfield

Clopton Church

Charsfield New Village Hall

New Village Hall at Charsfield, opened by Mrs P. Youngman, January 2001

Water Mill Cottages, Kettleburgh, refurbished 1999

Robins Nest, Dallinghoo, renovated 1999

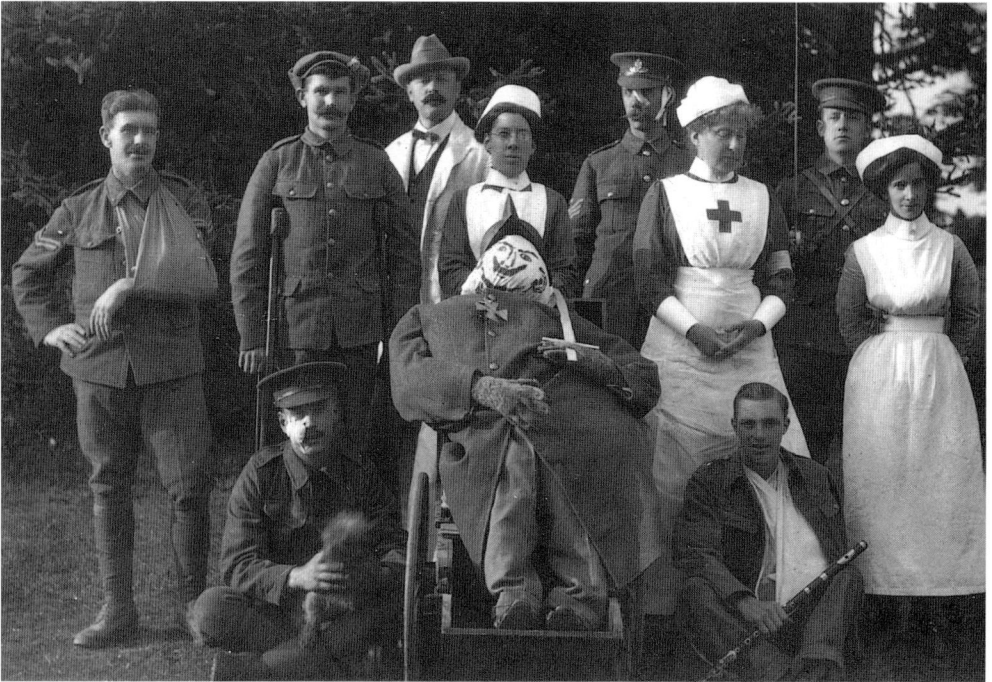

Guy Fawkes at Duke of Hamilton estate, Easton Park

Christmas 1915, Duke of Hamilton estate, Easton Park

Staff and patients at Easton Park

Wounded soldiers at Duke of Hamilton estate, Easton, March 1916

Back view of Easton park, taken down in 1920. At one time it used to be the front of the Mansion

Mr Fred Copping's wedding in Easton 1925

Quoit players – note the bicycle clips (Stebbings brothers of Otley and friends)

Peter Holloway, "Elvis Presley"

Peter Driver and Howard Felton, sand dancers

The Uplands, Easton – see thatched roof. Author lived here in childhood

The modern Uplands, Easton, 2000

Author's mother, aunt and grandmother

Author and brother Ronnie

Author's great-grandparents and family

Well-known horsemen, Ray Hubbard and Tom Warne

Dennis O'Brien-Baker, Martlesham Nurseries – famous for his Iceland Poppies – never missed as an exhibitor since Chelsea Flower Show started

The late Bertie Riches (Judge) and dog, of Melton

Wedding at Hoo – Canon D. Yates to K. Branton; I. Archer, best man, on left, P. Branton on right

David Thorndike taking his daughter Iris to her wedding 30th January, 1954

Mrs Kathleen Thorndike (David's wife) with her grand-daughter, Anna-Marie, 1969

The Stebbings family from Dallinghoo, Dennis and Ethel with Edna, Ted, Claude and Frank (about 1932)

Mrs Dennis Stebbings with her son Claude

Mrs Emily Stebbings with her daughter, Florence Elliott, her grand-daughter Mary Stewart, and her grandson Claude Stebbings

Mr and Mrs Dodger Stebbings and Kathleen Cole (Mrs B. Martin)

Bredfield Pump (Coronation sign made by Pearce's Blacksmiths)

The Adams family from Friday Street, Brandeston, Mrs K. Thorndike's family

Mrs Florrie Thorndike, Monewden

Kathy Fletcher, Charsfield

Mrs Warne, Monewden

The Mead Brothers – George, Fred and Will, Charsfield

Brian Archer, Charsfield, as a handsome baby

The Craig family, Home Farm, Dallinghoo, early 1940s

Bredfield Old Village Hall (old Army Hut) 1950s

Glevering Hall, near Wickham Market

Thistleton Hall, Burgh. Used to stand near Debach Airfield. Pulled down in 1955

The drawing room which contained wonderful wood panelling

Orford windmill. Came down in late 1920s

Mr & Mrs R. Pemberton wedding 1924, Charsfield

R. Pemberton with her Morris 1932 – 1955 at Charsfield

F. Taylor, J. Pemberton, M. M. Rowlands, F. Thurlow, R. Pemberton, D. Yates, on Charsfield tennis court, 1947

Woodbridge Flower Show 1912

D. Pemberton, H. Pemberton, E. Hammon, W. Martin, 1950

Judging Floral Ipswich – Peggy Cole, late Gordon Challacombe, late Arthur Borrett

The Hunt: Easton Harriers at Kettleburgh Chequers. Taken in early 1930s

Flooding at Kettleburgh, 1996

Flooding at Rackhams Mill, Wickham Market, 1996

Mrs Fox and staff who used to be cook at Sudbourne Hall

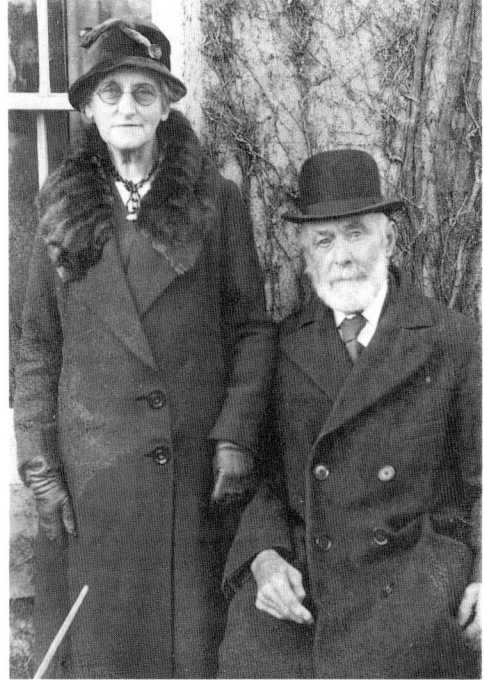

Golden wedding of Mr R. Pemberton's father and mother, mid 1930s

The Hall, Sudbourne, demolished 1952

The Shotley Motor Bus

Suffolk horses at Easton Farm Park